A Tail of Friendship

by Jamie Emlyn

Copyright © Jamie Emlyn 2025
All Rights Reserved
No part of this publication may be reproduced, distributed, or transmitted in any form or by any means, including photocopying, recording, or other electronic or mechanical methods, without the author's prior written permission, except in the case of brief quotations embodied in critical reviews and certain other non-commercial uses permitted by copyright law. For permission requests, please contact the author.

Dedications

Everything I do,
I do for one person - my daughter.

So to you Mya this book is dedicated,
my world - builder, with love.

Always. X

Acknowledgements

To Dennis, without whom
this book would not exist.
To Emma, for all her love and support,
and for getting me this far.
To Sophie, for her valuable advice.

In a cozy neighbourhood,
where the sun danced between leafy trees,
Dennis the cockerpoo lived with his family:
Dan, a kind-hearted graphic designer,
and his ten-year-old daughter, Mya.

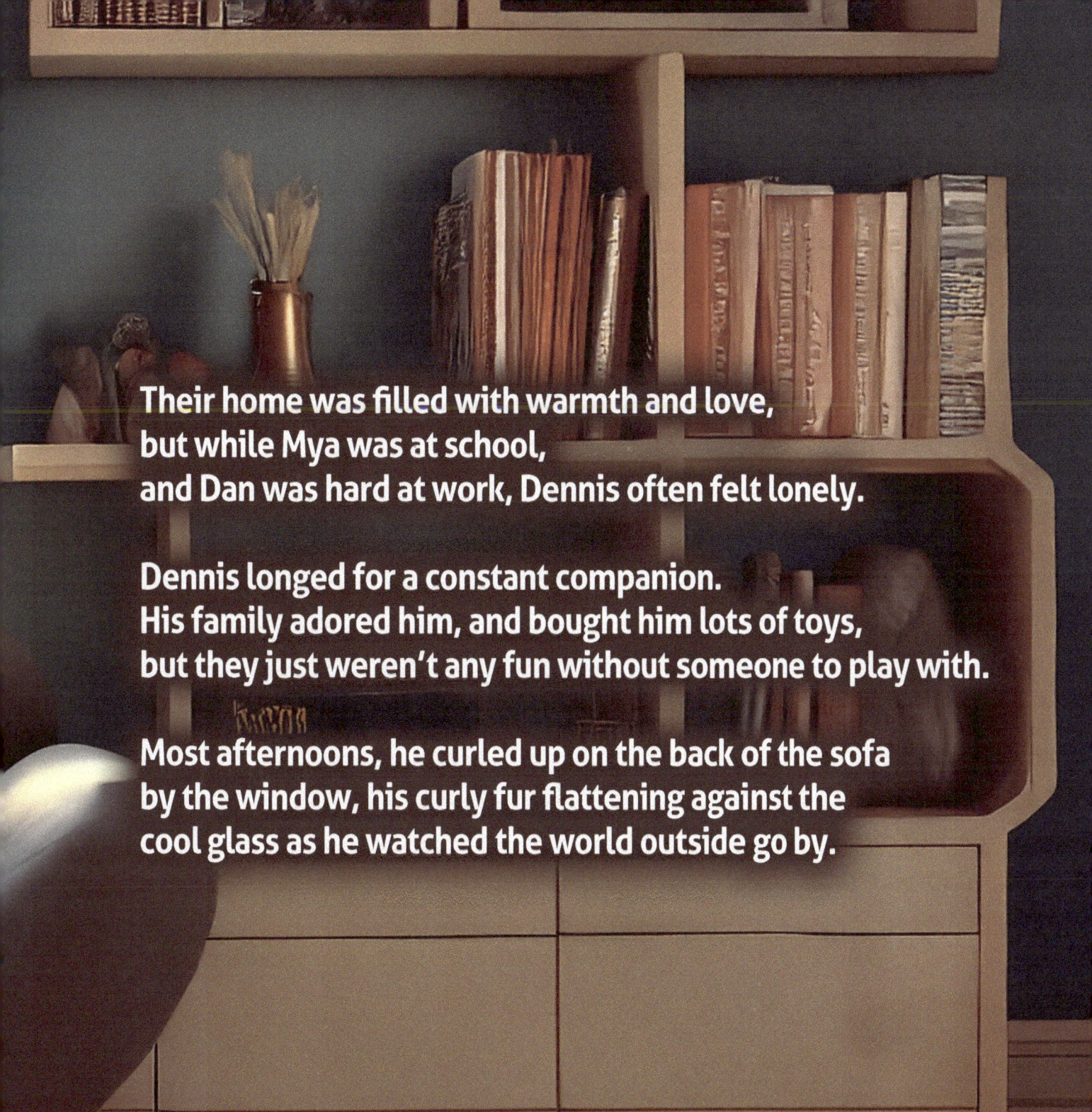

Their home was filled with warmth and love,
but while Mya was at school,
and Dan was hard at work, Dennis often felt lonely.

Dennis longed for a constant companion.
His family adored him, and bought him lots of toys,
but they just weren't any fun without someone to play with.

Most afternoons, he curled up on the back of the sofa
by the window, his curly fur flattening against the
cool glass as he watched the world outside go by.

He watched dogs chasing balls in the park, and wished he had a friend to play with.

Later that afternoon Dennis's ears perked up. It was the familiar sound of the front door opening.

"Dennis! I'm home!" Mya called, rushing over to hug him.

Dennis wagged his tail and nuzzled against her, soaking in the attention.

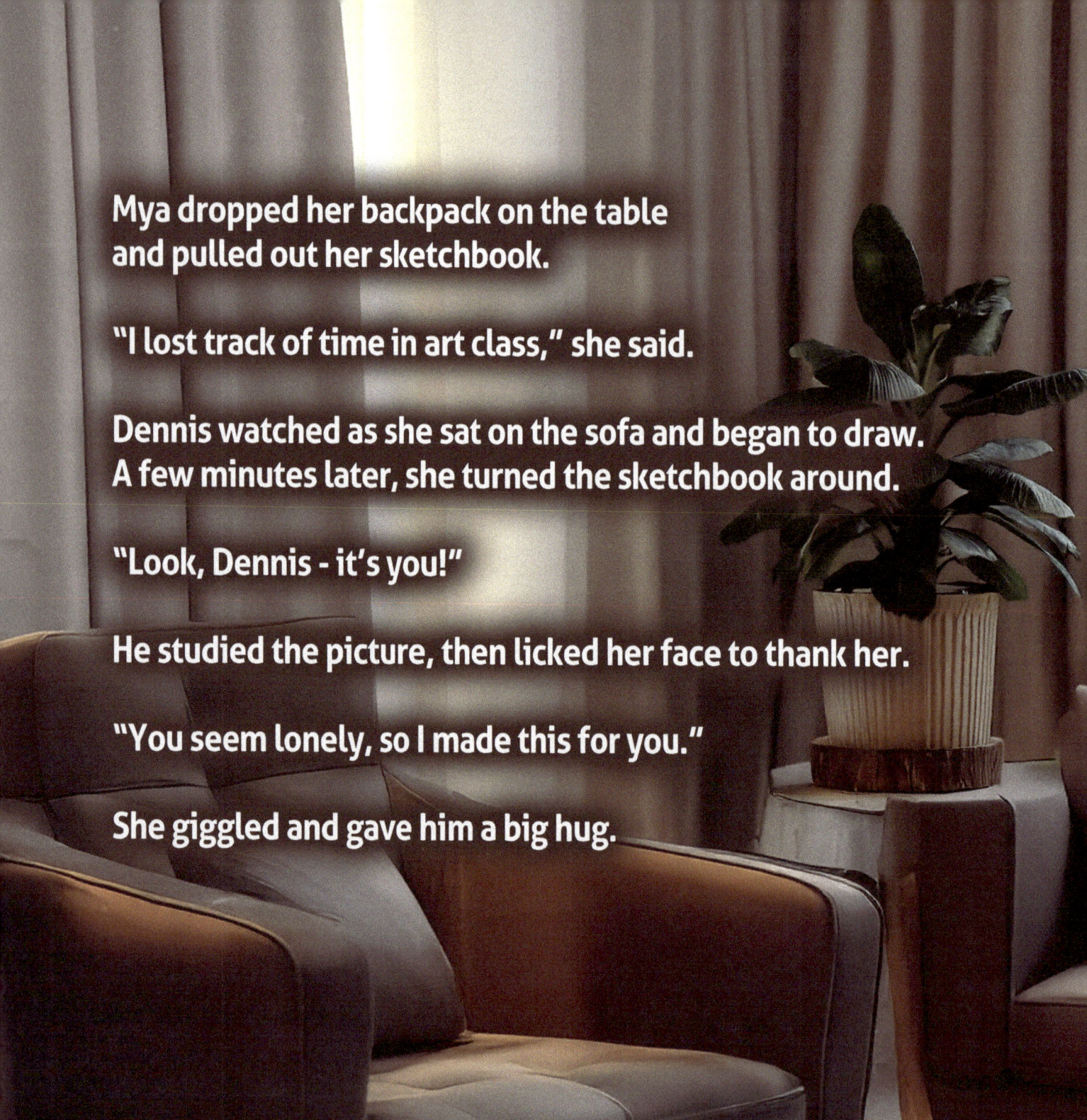

Mya dropped her backpack on the table and pulled out her sketchbook.

"I lost track of time in art class," she said.

Dennis watched as she sat on the sofa and began to draw. A few minutes later, she turned the sketchbook around.

"Look, Dennis - it's you!"

He studied the picture, then licked her face to thank her.

"You seem lonely, so I made this for you."

She giggled and gave him a big hug.

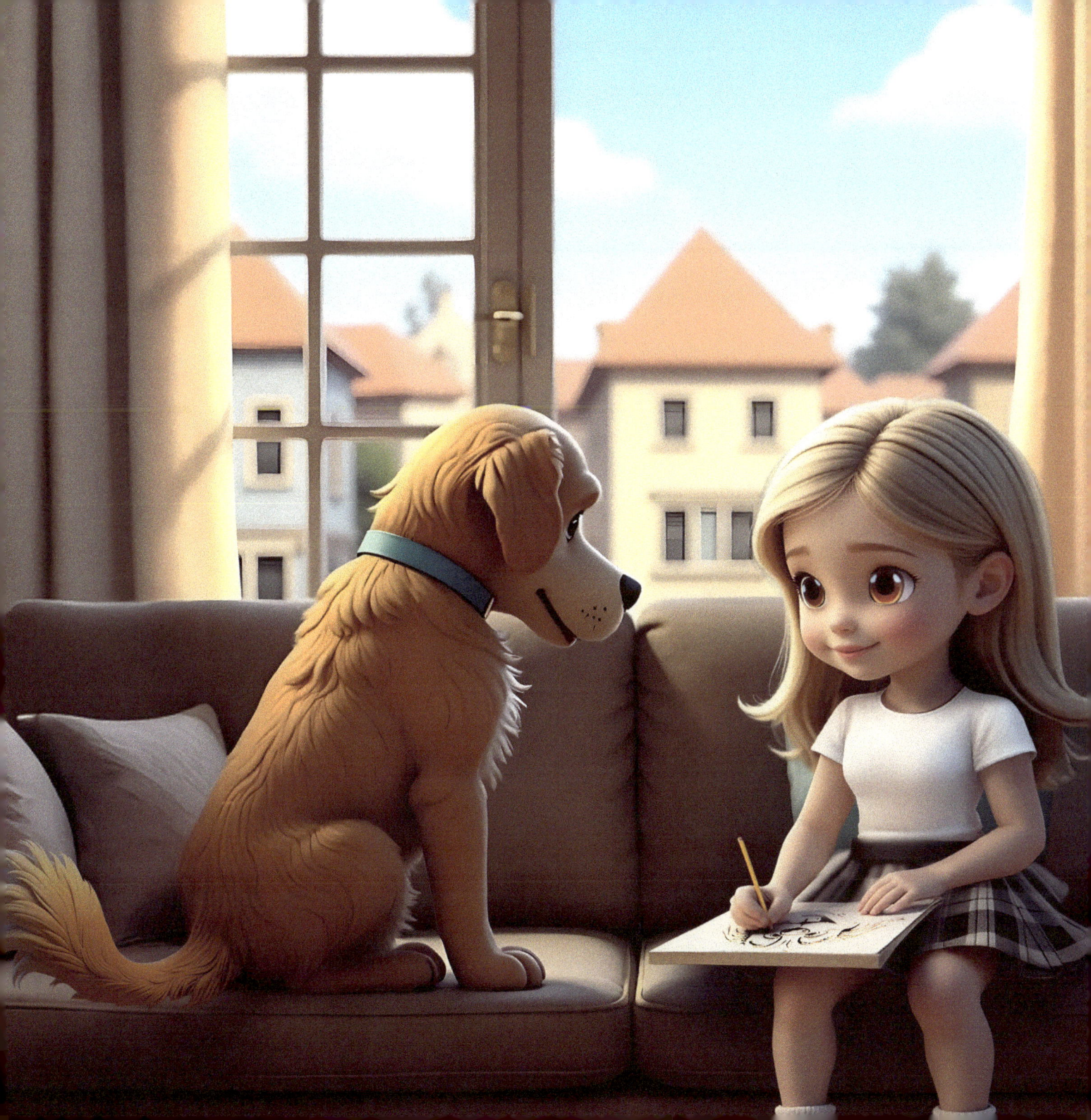

Then, an idea struck her.

"Let's go to the park and see who's there!"

At the sound of his lead jingling, Dennis sprang up in excitement. Mya clipped it onto his collar and, before stepping outside, she called to her dad,

"We're heading to the park, back in an hour!"

Dennis inhaled the fresh air as they walked. Mya chatted about her day, and Dennis stopped now and then to check out interesting smells.

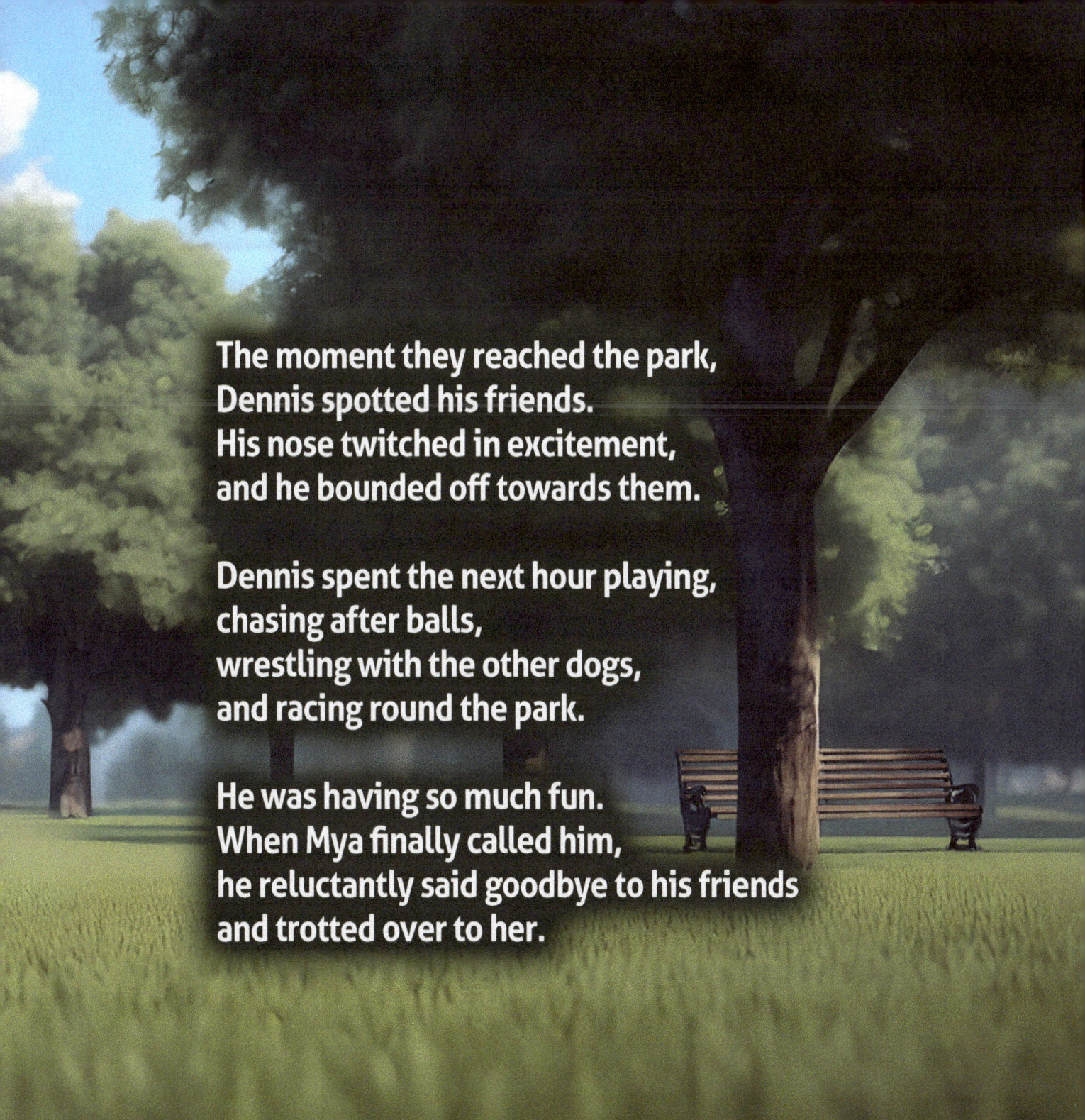

The moment they reached the park,
Dennis spotted his friends.
His nose twitched in excitement,
and he bounded off towards them.

Dennis spent the next hour playing,
chasing after balls,
wrestling with the other dogs,
and racing round the park.

He was having so much fun.
When Mya finally called him,
he reluctantly said goodbye to his friends
and trotted over to her.

After dinner, Dennis curled up on the sofa.
Dan was watching TV, and Mya was drawing in her book.
Mya looked down at Dennis and whispered...

"Love you, puppy. I'm so glad you're part of our family."

Later, Dennis felt lonely again, as Mya had started her homework and Dan was finishing his emails.

Dennis nudged his favourite squeaky toy, hoping someone would play, but the house was quiet.

He let out a big sigh and curled up on the rug.

One evening, Dan noticed Dennis gazing longingly out the window.
He knelt beside him, stroking Dennis's head,
"I think it's time we got you a friend," he said with a smile.

Dennis's ears perked up. A new friend?
His tail wagged furiously.
He imagined a little, fluffy puppy to chase balls with, snuggle up to, and play all day with.

Over the next few days,
Dennis watched as Dan brought home new supplies:
Food,
a bed,
a harness,
and some bowls.

But something puzzled him.
Everything was big. Bigger than his.
Shouldn't a little puppy need little things?

Finally, the big day arrived.
The door opened, and in walked Dan.
Dennis rushed forward,
ready to meet his new friend!

But instead of a bouncy little puppy...
In stepped Rosie. A regal Rottweiler
with sleek black fur and calm brown eyes.
And she was twice his size.

Rosie barely looked at him.
She just sat and watched the room.

Determined to make friends,
Dennis pranced around her,
wagging his tail and barking excitedly.

When she didn't react, he dashed off...
Returning with all his favourite toys,
laying them gently at her paws.

Still, Rosie didn't move.
So he ran to the garden, jumped behind the bushes,
and barked, hoping she'd join the game.

But the only sound was the rustling of leaves
beneath his paws.

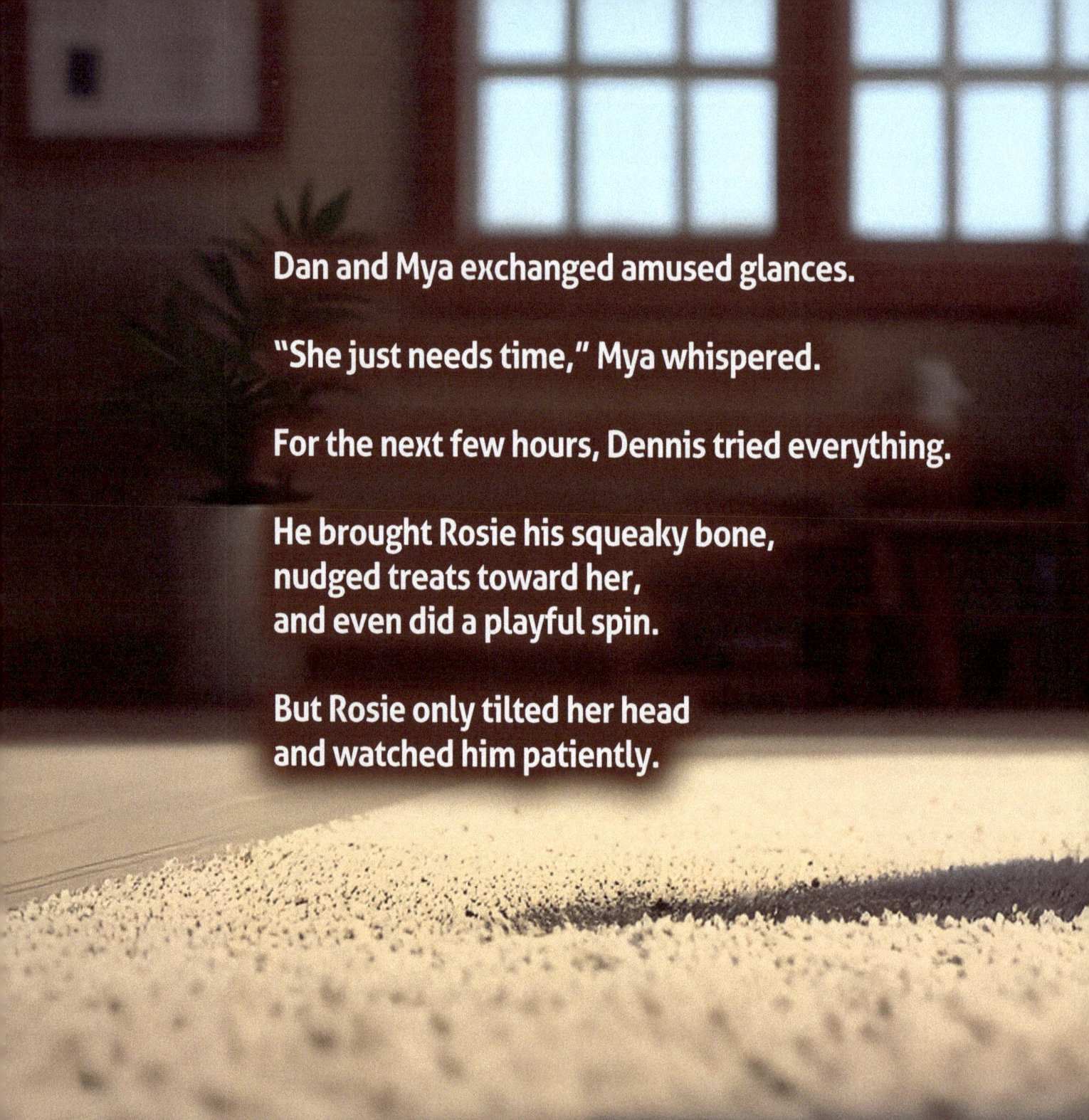

Dan and Mya exchanged amused glances.

"She just needs time," Mya whispered.

For the next few hours, Dennis tried everything.

He brought Rosie his squeaky bone,
nudged treats toward her,
and even did a playful spin.

But Rosie only tilted her head
and watched him patiently.

Dennis flopped onto the rug with a defeated sigh.
Maybe she didn't like him.
Maybe they weren't meant to be friends.

As he lay there, feeling sad,
he felt a soft nudge on his side.

He opened his eyes and saw Rosie standing over him.
She lowered her head and licked Dennis on his nose.

Then, to his surprise, she picked up a bright yellow ball
and dropped it in front of him.

Dennis's tail thumped on the floor.
Did this mean...?

He nudged the ball back.

Rosie stopped it and with a flick of her paw, pushed it gently to him.

Dennis leapt up with an excited bark.
They rolled the ball back and forth.

Then Dennis grabbed it and ran into the garden, looking over his shoulder...
Hoping she'd follow.

Rosie finally moved...

She chased after him,
her powerful strides graceful yet playful.

Dennis yapped with joy, zig-zagging through the garden.
All their differences faded, and there was only
the pure joy of running and chasing.
He no longer felt alone.

Dan and Mya watched from the porch,
smiling as the dogs played.

"I told you they'd be best friends."
Mya whispered.

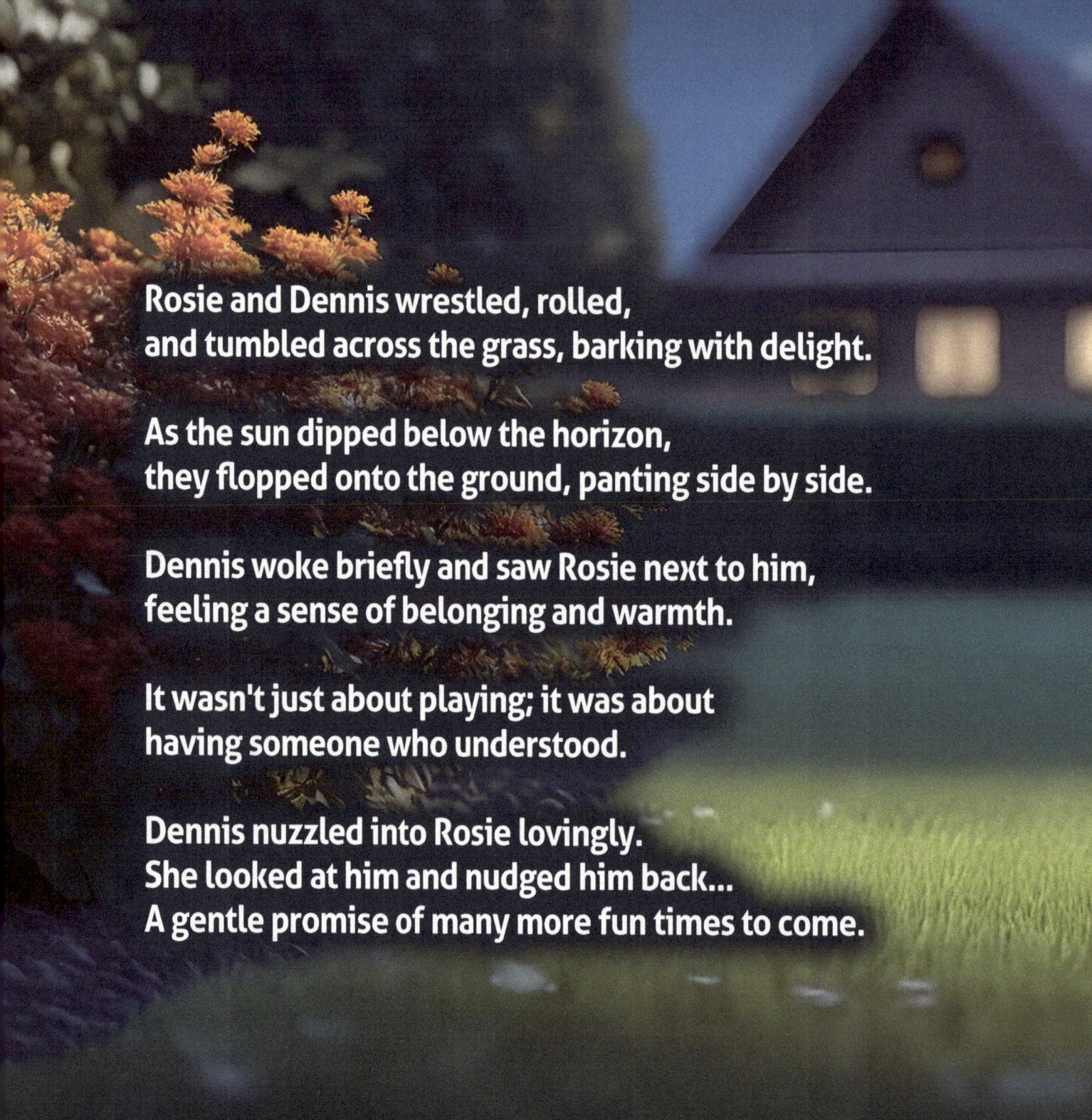

Rosie and Dennis wrestled, rolled,
and tumbled across the grass, barking with delight.

As the sun dipped below the horizon,
they flopped onto the ground, panting side by side.

Dennis woke briefly and saw Rosie next to him,
feeling a sense of belonging and warmth.

It wasn't just about playing; it was about
having someone who understood.

Dennis nuzzled into Rosie lovingly.
She looked at him and nudged him back...
A gentle promise of many more fun times to come.

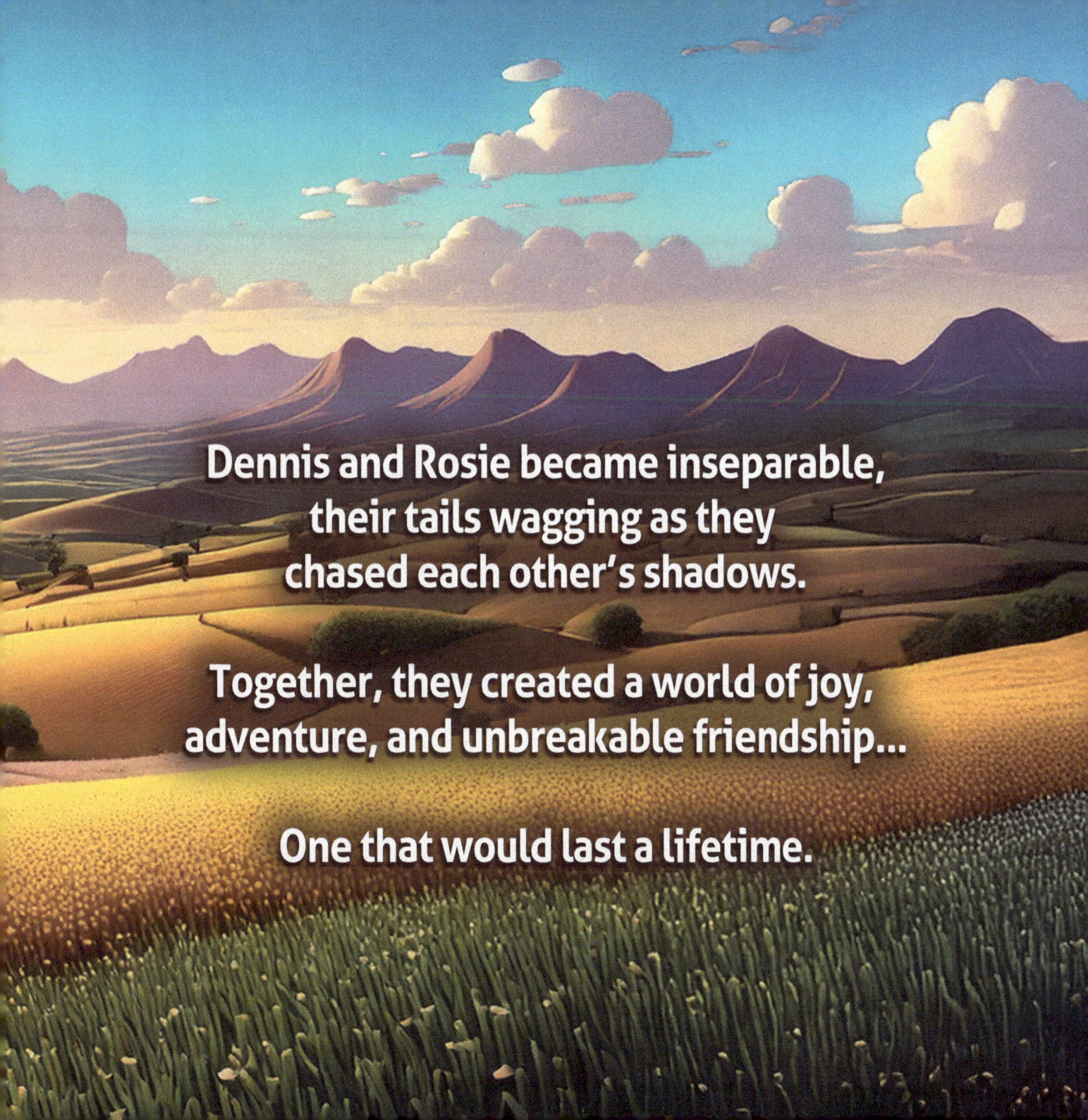

Dennis and Rosie became inseparable, their tails wagging as they chased each other's shadows.

Together, they created a world of joy, adventure, and unbreakable friendship...

One that would last a lifetime.

About the Author

Jamie Emlyn, the creator of Dennis's world, prefers their muse, Dennis the Cockerpoo (pictured), to take the spotlight. A graphic designer and qualified dog trainer, Jamie translates their love for canines into charming stories. Inspired by their own spirited dog, Dennis, and his protective cuddles, and by Dennis's friend Luna, who inspired the character of Rosie, Jamie, along with a close friend, embarked on this literary adventure to share the joy and camaraderie found in the bond between dogs and their human companions. Each character reflects the joy and companionship inherent in dog-human friendships. Jamie's tales celebrate the playful spirit and heartwarming bonds that make our four-legged friends so special.

Meet the Inspiration

Dennis

Rosie
(Luna)

www.ingramcontent.com/pod-product-compliance
Lightning Source LLC
Chambersburg PA
CBHW040044100526
44584CB00033BA/4268